DIARY OF A ~~BIG BAD~~ GOOD DINGO

DIARY OF A ~~BIG BAD~~ GOOD DINGO

INBALI ISERLES

JIM CRAWLEY

Collins

Contents

Fableland

The Wild Wood

Granny's Cottage

Jack's Beanstalk

Inn

Kiosk

Three Bears House

Mountain Pass

Southern Path

Gingerbread House

Prince Charming's Castle

2

ern Road

Merlin's House

River Pike

New Development

Mother
Goat's House

Police Station

Old
Road

Fernside Market

Farmer Ploddington's
Hen House

3

Chapter 1 Into the woods and far away

1st January:

Dear Diary,

Once upon a time, there was a wild dog called Dingo who left her village to seek her fortune in Fableland. And that wild dog is me! Hooray, it's a brand-new year! Here I am at the start of the Wild Wood. The trees are huge, reaching up to the sky. There are winding green vines *everywhere*. A veil of mist hangs over the Wild Wood. Sure, it looks a little gloomy, but I'm not scared.

I can't wait to find out what the future has in store. I'm all grown up and off on my very first adventure, and I'm hoping to make some friends along the way.

Better dash, I need to find some dinner.
I just spotted an old woman walking through
the woods. Maybe she knows a cafeteria ...

Wish me luck!

Dingo

5

1st January (later):

Dear Diary,

The old woman is lovely! She invited me to tea at her cottage. She told me to call her "Granny", and she called me "Lassie". That makes me sound like a tame dog. Granny said that she used to train dogs for the police ... I don't mind, I think I could get used to being her pet.

Granny is retired from the police. She told me that these days she's busy with "council duties". I'm not sure what that means. She also rents out a few houses in Fernside, east of the Wild Wood. The rest of the time, she likes to cook. She doesn't mind that I'm a vegetarian. She baked the most amazing carrot cake … it was delicious!

Dingo

ting form

DERN
IIDE
ENTISTRY

ALL THE BETTER
TO EAT
THINGS WITH

4th January:

Dear Diary,

I've had a brilliant few days with Granny. She's the best cook in the world! I don't want to criticise Dad or anything but his onion-skin pie is a bit chewy. Granny cooks vegetarian stews, and pasta, and the most incredible puddings.

I fixed a broken kitchen shelf. Granny was so happy!

 Dingo

6th January:

Dear Diary,

As we ate our cereal this morning, Granny told me that her sweet and clever granddaughter, Little Red Riding Hood, is coming to visit this weekend. Little Red wants to work for the police when she's grown up, just like Granny used to. Granny is sure she'll make an excellent police officer as she's *very* brave. Little Red is an animal lover too! I can't wait to meet her.

Granny plans to dress me up in one of her nighties as she says that I'll look super-cute that way, and Little Red will adore me. I think this sounds like a brilliant idea! Granny says that Little Red LOVES surprises.

I might even climb into Granny's bed and pretend to be her! That would be a fun surprise, wouldn't it, Diary? I hope Little Red is as good at baking as Granny …

It's getting late now so I'd better go to sleep. I can hear owls hooting outside in the Wild Wood, but I'm not scared.

Goodnight,

 Dingo

9th January:

Dear Diary,

Disaster! Little Red is TERRIFYING and NOT AN ANIMAL LOVER AT ALL. In fact, she must LOATHE dogs as she screamed when she saw me in Granny's bed. She's handy with a slingshot, and she took aim at me as I ran around and around the house. She caught my puffy tail! What's her problem?! She threatened to make me into a fur coat if I didn't get out of Granny's home, before chasing me into the Wild Wood.

No more carrot cake for me.

(OK, so I AM larger than other dogs. But she didn't need to overreact. I can't help my great big eyes, my great big ears and my lovely long white teeth.)

Now I am hiding under the leaves of
a giant beanstalk. A young man just walked by.
I said hello but he just glared at me and dashed
up the beanstalk. It's starting to get dark.
The Wild Wood is much scarier outside
Granny's cosy cottage.

What's that sound? Gulp ... I guess I'd
better find out ...

Dingo

12

Chapter 2 Who's been sitting in my chair?

9th January (later):

Dear Diary,

This afternoon, I heard footsteps in the Wild Wood. Small steps – like the feet of children. When I padded towards the sound, I couldn't see anyone. But I did make an interesting discovery: breadcrumbs were dotted along the grass, underneath the tall trees. It was almost like someone had put them there on purpose!

I followed the breadcrumbs, gobbling up each in turn. The very last one took me to a little wooden hut in the middle of the forest.

I had a peek through the window. No one was in, so I kept walking.

Breadcrumbs are fine but I'm going to need more to eat soon. I miss Granny's cooking.

 Dingo

12th January:

Dear Diary,

Well, it's been an interesting few days.
After I left the little wooden hut, I didn't see
a house for miles. Not a sausage! Oh, I mustn't
think about sausages, I'm hungry again
(I would only eat *vegetarian* sausages,
of course). At least I've had porridge – sorry,
I'm getting ahead of myself.

The Wild Wood was quite cheerful in
the sunshine. I wasn't scared anymore!
Songbirds were warbling in the trees.
Between a couple of oaks, a cottage appeared
like a mirage.

The first thing I noticed was that
the front door to the cottage was wide open.

I approached warily. After what happened
with Little Red Riding Hood, I wasn't taking
any chances. I knocked on the open door.
I could hear someone snoring inside, and I had
a look – why, it was only a girl! She had lovely
ringlets as yellow as dandelions, and she was
fast asleep on the smallest of three beds.

She woke up suddenly. I thought that the girl
might scream at me, just like Little Red.

Instead, she rubbed her eyes and yawned. "Do you live here?" she asked. I told her that I didn't. I was a bit surprised to be honest – if she was asking me that question, didn't that mean that *she* didn't live in the cottage? And if she didn't live there, why was she sleeping in the smallest bed?

"My name's Goldilocks," she told me. I told her I was Dingo. She invited me in and offered me a medium-sized bowl of porridge. She said we would be best friends.

I suppose it was a bit strange that she was offering me food when she didn't even live in the cottage (at least, I don't *think* she did). But I was too hungry to complain!

Goldilocks warned me that the porridge was cold, but I slurped it up happily. Let me tell you, Diary, it was *just right*.

There was also a large bowl of porridge and Goldilocks said I could eat that too. She warned me that it was a bit too hot, but I didn't mind. I guess I'm not very fussy!

PORRIDGE PORTION GUIDANCE

NOT TOO HOT OR TOO COLD!

After I'd finished my porridge, I noticed that there were two chairs next to the dining table. A third chair – much smaller than the others – was broken on the floor.

"Don't worry about that," said Goldilocks.

Goldilocks went back to the little bed, saying she was sleepy. She told me that I was welcome to take a nap too. She's such a good friend!

So here I am, Diary, curled up in the middle bed. There's a photo of a little brown bear in a small frame on the bedside table. I wonder about that photo – I mean, who keeps a photo of a bear cub? Never mind. It's been a tiring few days. This bed is SO comfy. I'll just shut my eyes for a few minutes …

 Dingo

12th January (later):

I woke up with a start to the sound of
a creaking door. It was cold and dark in
the room, with only the glow of the moon
through the windows. I turned to Goldilocks
but she wasn't in the little bed anymore.
She had disappeared!

"Who's been sitting in my chair?" boomed
a huge, grizzly voice ...

 Dingo

Chapter 3 The big bad

14th January:

Dear Diary,

Sorry I left you on a cliffhanger! I was sitting in the forest while I was writing that last entry, and I saw an old woman walking nearby. I'll get to that soon.

You're probably wondering who lived in the cottage, and what they did when they found me there in the middle bed.

THREE BEARS entered the cottage. I was so scared I could hardly breathe! I recognised Baby Bear from the bedside photo. Mummy Bear was huge. But Daddy Bear was the worst – he was ENORMOUS!

He demanded to know where the rest of my
pack was hiding. I told him I don't have a pack!

Then the bears noticed that Baby Bear's
chair was broken, and that their porridge
had been eaten. They seethed with anger!
Mummy Bear was shocked that I was sleeping
in her bed.

I hadn't realised! I said that I was VERY sorry, it was all a misunderstanding. I offered to fix the chair. I didn't mention Goldilocks, no point getting her into trouble.

Remember how I told you I'm handy at fixing things? As the bears watched, I hammered the little chair back together. I sanded it down, good as new. Better than new, if I say so myself.

The bears were overjoyed. Even Daddy Bear smiled as I left.

Soon I was back on the forest path. I saw someone ahead of me in the moonlight. It was an old woman – but it wasn't Granny. Her long silver hair flowed over a beige cape. She turned her head, and her eyes glowed ghostly yellow! I hid behind a tree until she'd passed.

The old woman looked frightening, but she smelt great. Like all dogs, I have a very sensitive nose. The old woman smelt *sweet*.

 Dingo

16th January:

Dear Diary,

The last two nights I've slept on a pile of leaves under a tree. I say I'm not scared of the Wild Wood, but it isn't true. There are creepy sounds here after dark. The hooting of owls, the whisper of the wind ... I wish I could go back to Granny's. I don't suppose I'll ever see her again. 🙁

Sorry to be gloomy, Diary. I feel like turning tail and going home, but I'm not a quitter!

🐾 Dingo

17th January:

Dear Diary,

Today I found a kiosk in the forest. Groups were gathered around tables, eating lunch. I could smell all sorts of interesting aromas, like grilled cheese. Yum! But as I neared the kiosk, people turned and screamed.

An old man and a boy started to run. I noticed that the boy was made of wood – like a puppet, but with no strings!

Only a young woman stayed at her seat.
She called me over. Her hair was as black
as coal, and her skin was as white as snow.
"Here, let me get you something to eat, you look
hungry," she said, in a tinkling voice. She insisted
on paying for my meal. The man in the kiosk
looked shocked when he handed over a vegetable
pie in return for the young woman's silver coin.

"Why is everyone scared of me?"
I asked her.

The young woman laughed. "Don't you know?
After all, you're the big bad – "

She didn't have a chance to finish her sentence.
Seven little men appeared between the trees.
They watched with worried faces. One of them
sneezed – maybe he's allergic to dogs!

The young woman winked at me, then she left.

I don't even know her name!

🐾 Dingo

17th January (later):

Dear Diary,

I felt better with a good meal inside me.
I went on through the Wild Wood and was
soon completely lost. I started to panic that
I wouldn't find the forest path, but then
I forgot about that because I picked up
the most amazing smell. So sweet! So delicious!
Familiar too ...

As I padded around a low bush, my
jaw fell open. Up ahead was a beautiful
gingerbread house. It was decorated all over
with real sweets!

 Dingo

Chapter 4 Good enough to eat

17th January (a bit later):

Dear Diary,

I've been sitting under a hedge watching the gingerbread house. The smell is incredible. Sugary-sweet marzipan, pear drops, toffee chews … I'm drooling! The house is as pretty as a picture. It should be the most welcoming place in the world. But something warns me that I shouldn't approach.

Remember the other day how I told you I could hear footsteps? Children's footsteps? Well, I can hear them again.

More soon!

 Dingo

17th January (much later):

While I hid under the hedge, two children walked out of the forest, a girl and a boy. They were complaining that they were lost, and muttering something about disappearing breadcrumbs. They gasped when they saw the gingerbread house. They ran towards it and started tearing off handfuls of sweets and stuffing them in their mouths. I wasn't sure they should be doing that …

I called out to warn them and they turned to me, sweets falling out of their mouths. The boy screamed. He started to back away from me. The door to the house swung open and an old woman came out – the same scary old woman I'd seen in the forest.

That's why the sweet smell hadn't seemed right to me. It was *her* smell.

"Don't go in!" I cried, but the woman with the ghostly yellow eyes ushered the children inside.

"Be gone, lupine beast!" she cried. I have no idea what she meant. Then she slammed the door shut.

Oh well, I suppose the children will be fine. Still, I'm not sure I'll ever look at gingerbread the same way.

They will be fine, won't they, Diary?

 Dingo

18th January:

Dear Diary,

What a strange day! I felt guilty leaving the children with that yellow-eyed woman. I started to think about going to the police. Maybe someone could pop into the gingerbread house to check everything is OK?

A short, bearded man was laughing to himself on the forest road.

"What do you want?" he snapped, as I approached. He looked very suspicious. I asked him for directions to the police station. "Do you want me to spin straw into gold for you?" he offered. What an odd thing to say!

"No thanks, just the police station."

The short man said he would show me the way if I could guess his name.

"Matty?" I asked. "Luca, Henry, Mo?"

The man shook his head, cackled, and skipped away.

 Dingo

21st January:

Dear Diary,

I've spent a few nights staying at an inn on the forest road. The innkeeper glares when he sees me but at least he's given me a room. I try to avoid the other guests. I've heard them whispering about some big ball at Prince Charming's palace. I don't have time for balls (not that I'd ever be invited).

I'm still on my way to the police station, but it's taking longer than I thought.

 Dingo

22nd January:

Dear Diary,

I'm feeling bad that I'm still at the inn. I should have left by now. Truth is, I want to go home. No one here is friendly.  I keep reminding myself that I'm not a quitter.

Hoping for a better day tomorrow.

 Dingo

23rd January:

Dear Diary,

Sorry I was so miserable yesterday. I feel upbeat today! I had a chat with a tiny man called Tom over breakfast at the inn. Tom was very talkative and didn't seem to be scared of me or anyone else, even though he's only the size of a human thumb! Like everyone else, he mostly spoke about Prince Charming's ball. But he also told me that the police station is only a few miles away. I'm off there this morning!

Dingo

23rd January (later):

Disaster! I just approached the police station and who did I see at the entrance? It was Little Red Riding Hood!!! She seems to be on work experience. Granny told me that Little Red wanted to be a police officer, didn't she?

I need to get out of this place!

🐾 Dingo

Chapter 5 Kidding around in Fernside

25th January:

Dear Diary,

You'll never believe it, but I met a wizard called
Merlin on the forest road! He'll let me sleep on
his sofa for a couple of nights.

Nice man. A bit absent-minded. He left a pot bubbling with potion, and it fizzed all over the place. Some of it ran over my tail and turned it a ghastly green! Merlin said to forget about the police. He doesn't like anyone to tell him what to do. He's working on a secret spell. He mentioned a legend and something called "Excalibur" but he didn't go into details.

Merlin told me that a WITCH lives in the gingerbread house. I panicked and started to leave – I have to get over my fear of Little Red Riding Hood and report what I saw to the police! But Merlin said there's no point and that I shouldn't worry. He has lots of magic, and is sometimes able to foretell the future. He says the girl in the witch's house is called "Gretel", and that she's going to overpower the witch.

He says that the children will be rich and happy.

Honestly, I'm not sure whether to believe him. It sounds a bit crazy! But then, he is a wizard. I suppose wizards understand witches better than the rest of us.

Merlin doesn't want me to stay too long. He has to work on his potions. I offered to be his apprentice, but he said that he prefers to work alone. I'll be back on the road again tomorrow, looking for a new home.

Dingo

29th January:

Dear Diary,

The oddest thing happened last night! I was walking on the forest road after dark in the direction of Fernside. I'm not a fan of the Wild Wood at night, but too many people scream when they spot me in daylight!

I passed an enormous palace, with pointed turrets and steps leading up to the grand front door. I heard music and glimpsed people in silk gowns dancing to an orchestra. It was Prince Charming's ball!

A young woman raced down the steps of the palace. She tripped and her glass slipper fell off! Then she jumped into a waiting horse-drawn coach.

45

As the coach set off, it seemed to be turning into a pumpkin. Is that even possible?!

Dingo

30th January:

Dear Diary,

Fernside is amazing! It's a big development with lots of houses and shops and cafeterias. I stood at the edge of a marketplace, watching from the shadows. The short, bearded man I met on the forest road was talking to a woman – remember him, Diary? The man who offered to spin straw into gold. I could hear him saying that Mother Goat had just moved into town with her seven kids.

He said that Mother Goat had rented a house from the Leader of Fernside Council. "The Councillor owns half of Fernside," he told the woman.

The woman tutted. "Those houses aren't worth the money," she said. "Bits and pieces keep going wrong. They need a caretaker for repairs."

"I'd hate that job," said the little man.

Oh Diary, I would LOVE that job. But no one would employ a wild dog.

 Dingo

30th January (later):

Dear Diary,

I've had a great idea! I'm going to call on Mother Goat to see if she and her kids would like to join me for dinner. They're new to Fernside, and I'm an outsider too. I'm sure they would love a new friend.

I've got a really good feeling about this.

Dingo

30th January (much later):

Dear Diary,

That didn't go how I thought it would.
I knocked on Mother Goat's door. The door
didn't open, but I'm sure I heard the clip-clop
of small hooves. I knocked louder. I called out
in my nicest voice, "Hello, little goats, won't
you open the door? I would love to have you
for dinner!"

"Go away!" squeaked a voice – it must have
been a kid. He threatened to call the police!

Nobody likes me.

Dingo

Chapter 6 Fixing things

31st January:

Dear Diary,

I've been having a Big Think. I'm not a quitter, really I'm not. But I've decided it's time to go home. I don't have a job. I haven't made any friends, not really. I thought Goldilocks was my friend, but she ran away when the three bears came home. A real friend wouldn't do that, would they? She left me to face those angry bears on my own!

The people in Fernside don't want me here any more than the people I met in the Wild Wood. They seem to have something against me!

Maybe they just don't like strangers.
I'm planning to leave in the morning.

I'm not a quitter, but I QUIT.

 Dingo

1st February:

Dear Diary,

So this is it, my final day in Fernside. I used the last of my money to get a sandwich from a wary woman at the market. It's lonely being in a new place when no one will talk to you.

The closest I had to a real friend was Granny. I'd better remember to avoid Granny's cottage when I pass through the Wild Wood, just in case her granddaughter is visiting her. That's a shame, isn't it, Diary? I keep wondering if there's a way I could keep in touch with Granny, but how can I? I don't want to be made into a fur coat!

If I follow the southern path, I should be safe.

 Dingo

1st February (later):

Dear Diary,

HELP!!! I spoke too soon – I just saw Little
Red Riding Hood striding through Fernside.
She was holding her slingshot with a big frown
on her face. She looked so angry that a vein
was standing out on her forehead! I heard
her asking the woman from the marketplace if
she'd seen a "large, furry, dangerous predator".
I think she meant me!!!

I'll have to sneak past her.

 Dingo

1st February (much later):

Dear Diary,

It's been quite a day. I hardly know where to begin! Unluckily, my sneaking wasn't good enough. As I tried to scramble past Little Red, staying veiled in the shadows so she wouldn't see me, I heard a squeal. Mother Goat pointed a hoof at me. "It's just as my kids told me! There he is!"

I'm not even a "he"! I'm a girl! Well, Little Red must have heard Mother Goat as she started striding towards me.

All the people in the marketplace turned to look. There was the short, bearded man (with the secret name), and the woman from the marketplace, and I'm sure I spotted Goldilocks in the crowd.

Mother Goat kept shouting about me trying to eat her kids. I told her that I was a vegetarian but she wouldn't listen!

Little Red raised her slingshot. "You're coming with me to Prince Charming's jail."

Just then, a great booming voice rang out. "Little Red Riding Hood, you stop that *at once*!"

Everyone turned to look across the marketplace. I heard someone whisper, "It's the Councillor of Fernside!" People stood to attention respectfully and the crowd parted to let someone through.

Can you guess who it was, Diary?

It was Granny!!! GRANNY IS LEADER OF THE FERNSIDE COUNCIL! She also owns lots of houses which she rents out, like the one where Mother Goat lives with her kids. Well, Granny gave Little Red quite the ticking off, let me tell you. She pointed out that I am a *dog* (she still thinks I'm the tame kind of dog, but never mind).

Everyone had thought I was some terrible hunter on the loose. It's all been a case of mistaken identity!

Granny was so happy to see me! She told me that she was lonely when I left. She offered me a permanent home at her cottage AND a job as a caretaker for her Fernside houses. I get to fix them and make them run like clockwork. It's my dream job!

I've made loads of new friends. The people here are lots of fun when you get to know them! There's no big bad predator in Fableland. The sun is shining, the future is bright.

I feel quite *sure* that we'll all live happily ever after. (")

 Dingo

Fairy-tale characters

1 Granny and Little Red Riding Hood 2 Jack
3 Goldilocks and the Three Bears 4 The witch from
Hansel and Gretel 5 Snow White and the Seven Dwarfs
6 Hansel and Gretel 7 Merlin 8 Rumpelstiltskin
9 Tom Thumb 10 Cinderella 11 Prince Charming
12 Mother Goat and the Seven Young Goats 13 Pinocchio

Is that everyone? Or has someone escaped our attention...?

Real life dingoes

What exactly are dingoes?

Dingoes are wild dogs that live in Australia and parts of Southeast Asia.

Dingoes are the largest land predators in Australia. They hunt small animals such as birds, rabbits, lizards and fish. Although they gladly eat berries and vegetables, in reality, they are not likely to be vegetarians like Dingo in the story.

Do dingoes live in forests, like the Wild Wood?

Dingoes can survive in a range of different places. They can live in forests and also grasslands and deserts. Dingoes howl to each other and make other sounds like growling and whining.

Fernside Gazette

9p

1st April

Dingo's quick thinking saves Fernside home

Local hero Dingo got a special award today! She saved Mother Goat's house when the River Pike burst its banks. Dingo surrounded the house with sandbags, and pumped water away from the front door. Her quick thinking meant the house stayed dry.

"Dingo saved the day!" said Mother Goat, cuddling her seven young kids.

65

FERNSIDE NOTICE BOARD

Dingo's DIY
– satisfaction guaranteed

Need help fixing that fence?

Shoddy shelves causing you headaches?

Don't worry, Dingo's DIY can do the job!

For the best rates in Fernside,

call Woof-700

7-A-SIDE FOOTBALL TEAM NEEDED
Urgent start!
Happy, sleepy, grumpy, sneezy, bashful,
dopey and doc(tor) players welcome

MISSING!

ARTIST IMPRESSION ←

Hens missing from henhouse

Fernside Police are investigating the disappearance of 12 hens from Farmer Ploddington's Chicken Farm. "Whoever got in there was clever and strong," said Farmer Ploddington. "If I didn't know better, I'd think Big Bad was back."

eed a house-sitter?

Call GOLDILOCKS on GOLDI-600

(I may eat your porridge)

Jack's MAGIC BEANS

Best In fableland

*may cause unwanted visits by giants

Little Red Riding Hood's diary

31st March

Dear Diary,

OK, so I got it wrong about Dingo. She's actually a nice dog, good at mending stuff, not a hunter at all, as it turns out. But I KNOW I was right about trouble in Fableland. Someone is up to no good. That business with Farmer Ploddington's hens, for example. Everyone's blaming Mr Fox, but I have my suspicions. I know who's really to blame.

He's back, isn't he, Diary? I feel it in my red cape. I feel it in my hood. I feel it in my BONES.

My slingshot is ready. I rarely miss.

This isn't over.

Little Red

About the author

Why did you want to be an author?

I always loved stories from the youngest age. On long hot summers when we stayed with my grandparents, my sister and I used to write and illustrate books. The books featured naughty kittens, and a magical wonderland hidden deep in the woods behind my grandparents' house.

Inbali Iserles

My spelling was (and still is) terrible and my handwriting was (and still is) pretty hard to read – but storytelling was something I can't remember ever living without!

How did you get into writing?

I never expected to be an author. I was actually training to be a lawyer when I started writing my first book, *The Tygrine Cat*. I began to picture an ancient war between feline tribes. When I still felt excited about the idea a few weeks later, I realised I would have to write the story.

What is it like for you to write?

I love worldbuilding – coming up with magical environments and characters who live in them.
For me, plotting is the most difficult part of the process.
Editing isn't as hard as plotting, but it takes a lot of time.
Actually writing is the quick bit!

What book did you love when you were young?
I absolutely loved the Moomin books, like *A Comet in Moominland*.

Why did you decide to write this book?
We grow up on fairy tales and their familiar characters: Goldilocks and the Three Bears, Little Red Riding Hood and Cinderella. I loved the idea of a story that explored the world of these characters and a case of mistaken identity!

Is there anything in this book that relates to your own experiences?
Dingo stands out like a sore thumb, and I know just how that feels. We moved around when I was a kid, and starting new schools was scary. My unusual name didn't help either! I worried that I didn't quite fit, just like Dingo.

What fairy-tale character would you like to be?
I think it would have to be fairy tale witch — one who gets away with it, of course! It would be amazing to have magical powers.

Why did you have a dingo for the main character?
I saw dingoes at a wildlife park when I was in Australia. They are big and beautiful wild. I started to ponder the idea of a story where a sweet-natured dingo was confused with that legendary biggest and baddest of baddies — you know the one! What could possibly go wrong?

About the illustrator

What made you want to be an illustrator?

Ever since I was young, I've always been fascinated with creating stories and drawing characters. I wondered "what job can allow me to do that every day?" And so here I am, illustrating as a job and creating stories and characters every day as a grown up!

Jim Crawley

How did you get into illustration?

I started by practising A LOT! I drew most of the time and got together a portfolio of characters, places and people. I sent this to lots of publishers and illustration agencies – sometimes hearing back, sometimes not, but I kept going. I think that is the key – keep going and believe in yourself and you will make it!

What did you like best about illustrating this book?

It was great to put a different spin on some well-known and beloved fantasy/fairy tale characters.

What was the most difficult thing about illustrating this book?

The most difficult thing was all the teeny, tiny details and trying to make sure the characters looked the same.

Is there anything in this book that relates to your own experiences?

I think Dingo's general sense of adventure and exploration really resonates with me as she wanted to "get out there" and explore new places. I've done that quite a bit in my life. I love new challenges and adventures.

Which of the characters do you like best? Why?

I really love Dingo and her travels through the Wild Wood, but I also really like Mother Goat and her seven kids. It made me laugh drawing these characters. As a dad myself I know how challenging one child can be, let alone seven!

Did you have to do any research about dingos? What did you find out?

When I was younger I really, really wanted a pet dingo with a red tie around its neck (this is why our dingo in the story has one!). I couldn't keep one as a pet as they are wild dogs, but unlike dogs they don't bark, they howl. Maybe this is why everyone mistook Dingo for someone else ...

Do you think fairy tales are still meaningful for people today? Why?

I think they are as they put a bit of magic and mystery into our lives! The characters in fairy tales are all relatable to us and they always have challenges or problems to solve and overcome, which I think we all have to do in the "real world" sometimes.

Book chat

Which part of the book did you like best, and why?

Dingo is mistaken for another character from fairy tales. Do you know who?

Is there a villain in this story? Explain your answer.

Does the book remind you of any other books you've read? How?

If you had to choose a character to play from the book, who would you choose and why?

Would you want to be friends with Dingo if you met her? Why?

Why do you think Little Red seems not to like Dingo?

Can you think of three words to describe Dingo's character?

Do you think Dingo changed between the start and the end of the story? If so, how?

Book challenge:

Write your own diary entry from a character in the book.

Collins
BIG CAT

Published by Collins
An imprint of HarperCollins*Publishers*
The News Building
1 London Bridge Street
London SE1 9GF
UK

Macken House
39/40 Mayor Street Upper
Dublin 1
D01 C9W8
Ireland

10 9 8 7 6 5 4 3 2 1

ISBN 978-0-00-862470-5

British Library Cataloguing-in-Publication Data

A catalogue record for this publication is available
from the British Library.

Download the teaching notes and
word cards to accompany this book at:
http://littlewandle.org.uk/signupfluency/

Get the latest Collins Big Cat news at
collins.co.uk/collinsbigcat

Author: Inbali Iserles
Illustrator: Jim Crawley (Astound Illustration
    Agency)
Publisher: Lizzie Catford
Product manager and
    commissioning editor: Caroline Green
Series editor: Charlotte Raby
Development editor: Catherine Baker
Project manager: Emily Hooton
Content editor: Daniela Mora Chavarría
Phonics reviewer: Rachel Russ
Copyeditor: Sally Byford
Proofreader: Gaynor Spry
Typesetter: 2Hoots Publishing Services Ltd
Cover designer: Sarah Finan
Production controller: Katharine Willard

Collins would like to thank the teachers and
children at the following schools who took part in
the trialling of Big Cat for Little Wandle Fluency:
Burley And Woodhead Church of England Primary
School; Chesterton Primary School; Lady Margaret
Primary School; Little Sutton Primary School;
Parsloes Primary School.

MIX
Paper | Supporting
responsible forestry
FSC™ C007454

Acknowledgements
The publishers gratefully acknowledge the
permission granted to reproduce the copyright
material in this book. Every effort has been made
to trace copyright holders and to obtain their
permission for the use of copyright material.
The publishers will gladly receive any information
enabling them to rectify any error or omission at th
first opportunity.

p62–63 Pawel Papis/Shutterstock, p70 author image
© Richard Mansell.